WILLIAM WALTON

SYMPHONY NO. 1

Study Score

EDITED BY
DAVID LLOYD-JONES

MUSIC DEPARTMENT

OXFORD
UNIVERSITY PRESS

OXFORD
UNIVERSITY PRESS

Great Clarendon Street, Oxford OX2 6DP, England
198 Madison Avenue, New York, NY 10016, USA

Oxford University Press is a department of the University of Oxford.
It furthers the University's aim of excellence in research, scholarship,
and education by publishing worldwide

Oxford is a registered trade mark of Oxford University Press
in the UK and in certain other countries

7 9 10 8 6

ISBN 978-0-19-368325-9

Music origination by Chris Hinkins

PREFACE

After the enthusiastic reception of his Viola Concerto of 1929 and the even greater success two years later of the cantata Belshazzar's Feast, it was clearly going to be only a matter of time before William Walton embarked on the challenge of a symphony. A powerful incentive to start work on one came after a fine performance of the concerto in January 1932 in Manchester, when Sir Hamilton Harty invited the composer to write a symphony for his Hallé Orchestra. Walton began the composition of the symphony in March 1932 and, for the first six months, progress was very slow. By the autumn he was living in Ascona, Switzerland, with Baroness Imma Doernberg, the attractive young widow with whom he had an on and off relationship for the next two years, and to whom the symphony was eventually dedicated. Work now became more productive, and on his return to London in the spring of 1933 the composer was able to play the completed first and second movements to his friends.

The slow movement (which originally contained an extended middle section recalling the malevolent mood of the Scherzo) was written fairly quickly and, by September, Walton was sketching the opening and coda of the last movement, though very soon he reached an impasse over suitable material for its main central section. Instead of persevering with it, Walton decided to use his time by orchestrating the three completed movements.

In the autumn of 1934, the London Symphony Orchestra (of which Harty was now Principal Conductor) announced that the orchestra would give a first performance of the three extant movements on 3 December at Queen's Hall. Walton had been subjected to a degree of pressure before eventually agreeing to this highly unorthodox procedure, but the success of the resulting performance justified the gamble that had been taken. He then resumed work on the last movement, and this was eventually completed on 30 August 1935.

The eagerly awaited first performance of the complete work was given at Queen's Hall by the BBC Symphony Orchestra under Harty on 6 November 1935, and was received with the greatest enthusiasm by the public and critics alike. Barely a month later, Harty recorded the symphony for Decca with his London Symphony Orchestra; at that time, a highly unusual honour for a new British work.

In the spring of 1936, Oxford University Press published the symphony in the form of full score, miniature score, and orchestral parts. These were soon discovered to contain a number of mistakes and inconsistencies and, over the years, efforts were made to correct them. In 1951, Walton conducted the Philharmonia Orchestra in his only recording of the work. For this occasion, he undertook a rigorous re-examination of the material, and also made a few new adjustments. Unfortunately, these were only entered into the parts, so that doubts immediately arose as to which was correct: the (unrevised) full score or the newly corrected parts. A 1968 reprint of the symphony in study score format, marked 'corrected 1968', improved matters considerably, but still left a significant number of errors.

For my new edition of the full score, which was published as Volume 9 of the William Walton Edition in 1998, I tried to arrive at an accurate and practical text that represented Walton's final wishes prior to his death in 1983. For this purpose, I was able to consult the autograph, copies of the 1951 'Walton set' of orchestral parts, and other appropriate sources.

The work itself, scored for a modest orchestra that is hardly larger than that required for Beethoven's Ninth Symphony, remains unique in twentieth century British music for its dramatic, virile, passionate, and expressive qualities, and represents the very summit of Walton's achievement.

David Lloyd-Jones, 2002

A fuller version of this Preface, together with detailed textual notes, can be found in Volume 9 of the William Walton Edition.

ORCHESTRATION

2 Flutes (second doubling Piccolo)

2 Oboes

2 Clarinets

2 Bassoons

4 Horns

3 Trumpets

3 Trombones

Tuba

Timpani (2 players. The second plays in the fourth movement only (fig. 137))

Percussion (2 players: Cymbals, Snare drum, Tam-tam. These play in the fourth movement only
(fig. 137))

Strings

Duration: *c.* 43 minutes

The first three movements of this symphony were performed by the London Symphony Orchestra in
Queen's Hall, London on 3 December 1934. The work was first performed in its entirety at a BBC
Symphony Concert in Queen's Hall on 6 November 1935. Both performances were conducted by Sir
Hamilton Harty.

to the Baroness Imma Doernberg

SYMPHONY No. 1

I

WILLIAM WALTON

48

629
Fl. 1 2
Ob. 1 2
Cl. 1 (B♭) 2
(a 2)
Fag. 1 2
(a 2)
Cor. (F) 1 2
3 4
Tr. (C) 1 2
3
1
f
Tbn. 1 2
a 2
ff
mf
Tbn. 3
Tba.
Timp.
ffz
Vln. I
Vln. II
Vle.
(div.)
Vcl.
unis.
Cb.

II

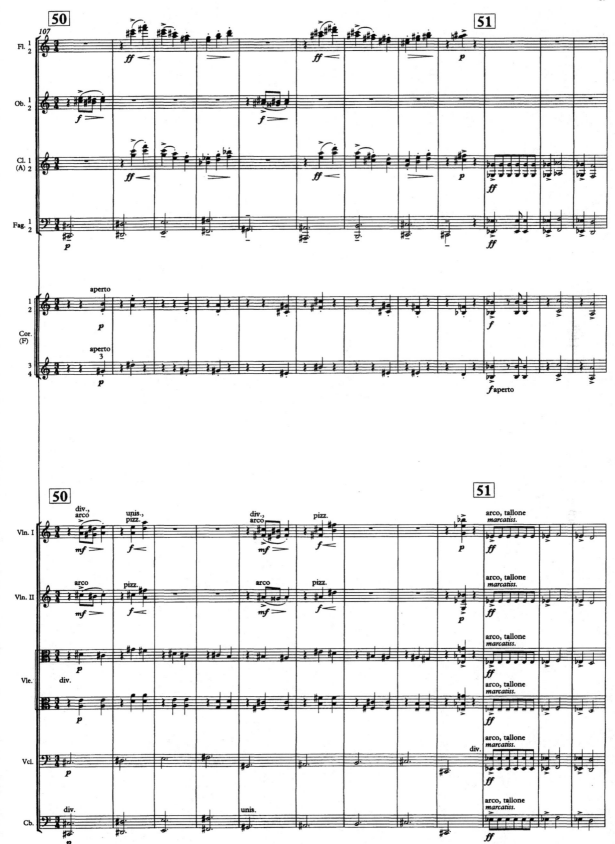

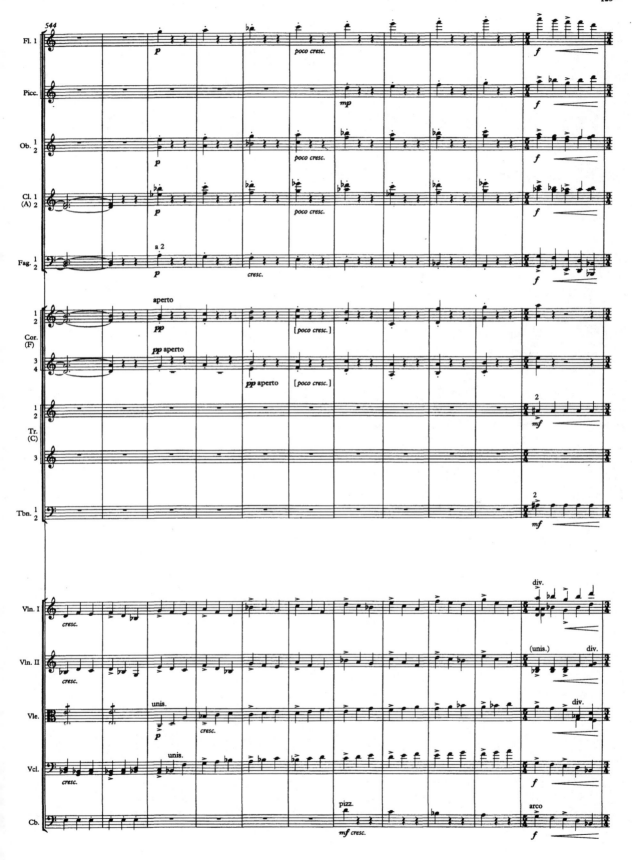

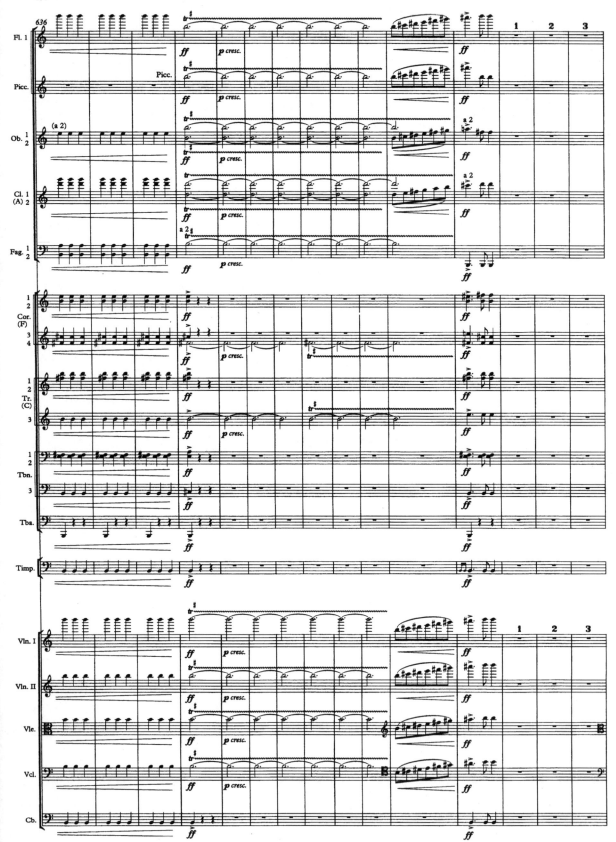

III

IV

128

139